Judy Blume's Story

Judy Blume's Story

by Betsy Lee

Dillon Press
New York

Collier Macmillan Canada
Toronto

Maxwell Macmillan International Publishing Group
New York   Oxford   Singapore   Sydney

Macmillan Publishing Company, 866 Third Avenue
New York, NY 10022

Printed in the United States of America

12   13   14   15   16   17

Library of Congress Cataloging in Publication Data

Lee, Betsy, 1949-
    Judy Blume's Story

    SUMMARY: A biography of Judy Blume, perhaps the most popular writer of juvenile fiction today, based on first hand information from the writer herself.
    1. Blume, Judy—Biography—Juvenile Literature. 2. Novelists, American—20th century—Biography—Juvenile literature. [1. Blume, Judy. 2. Authors, American] I. Title.
PS3552.L843Z75   813'.54   [B]   [92]   81-12494
ISBN 0-87518-209-7   AACR2

To my daughter, Brenna
May we always be friends.

Contents

Chapter 1

Just a Regular Kid

Splash. Judy closed her eyes as a wet sponge slapped her face. With a flurry of hands and brushes and sponges, the make-up man leaned over her, penciling her eyebrows, dusting her cheeks. Judy opened her eyes and glanced in the big Hollywood mirror. She looked glamorous.

Sometimes Judy felt as if she was living out a fantasy from her childhood. Had she really become a star? In the last few years her fame as a best-selling author had skyrocketed. She was a celebrity now, about to be interviewed on national television.

Psssst. The make-up man sprayed Judy's face so that her cheeks wouldn't glow with sweat under the high intensity lights. Minutes later she was sitting on stage in the "Today" show studio. Before the camera reached her, a tiny mike was clipped to her lapel. She tried not to notice the cameras and cables and bright lights hovering overhead. "Relax," she told herself. "Act natural."

The TV host turned to her and smiled. "Today we're talking to Judy Blume, the popular author of children's books, who has come out with a new book, *Superfudge*. It's not about a Fudgesicle out of control. This book is for your youngest readers."

"Yes," said Judy, "to make them laugh. I enjoy nothing better than hearing a kid laugh while reading a book."

Glancing now and then at his notes, the interviewer jumped quickly from question to question. He asked about the other books she had written and about her life as a writer. Judy thought of all the kids watching on television. She pretended she was sitting in their living room, talking to them face to face. That made her forget about the cameras and bright lights.

"You are living in Santa Fe," said the TV host. "You were raised in the East. Is there any difference between kids in the East and West?"

"Not really. Being a kid is a universal joy and a universal problem."

"You are forty-two. Does it bother you to talk about that?"

"Oh, no. I think it's very important. When I tell young people that I'm forty-two, they say, 'You are? That sounds so old.' I say, 'But it feels fine.' "

"Are you going to change your life?"

"Sure. Life is always changing. If it wasn't going to change, what would be the point of going on?"

"Judy Blume, nice to have you with us." The TV host smiled again as the camera switched from Judy's face to his. "Be back in just a few minutes, but first a station break." Judy breathed a sigh of relief. Walking off stage, she hurried to another interview.

"Life is always changing," she had said. Judy's life had changed more than she could have ever imagined. To the boys and girls who grew up with her in Elizabeth, New Jersey, Judy was just a regular kid who lived in a brick house on Shelley Avenue.

Judy was born in Elizabeth, New Jersey, on February 12, 1938. Her parents, Dr. Rudolph and Esther Sussman, had also been born and raised in Elizabeth. They had known each other since they were teenagers and had married when Dr. Sussman graduated from dental school. Judy was two years old when the Sussmans moved into their house on Shelley Avenue. She was so small that she had to reach to touch the tabletops. To a toddler, the house seemed very, very big.

On the first floor there was a big living room with a fireplace, a dining room, and a sun parlor. The upstairs had four bedrooms, a bathroom, and a closed-in porch that ran the whole length of the house.

The porch was called a sun deck because it was walled with windows. The sun bathed it with light and warmth in winter as well as summer. On rainy days Judy would spend hours there, playing with her dolls. The pattering of the rain on the frosted glass made a kind of soft, staccato music that drifted in and out of her mind as she lost herself in a fantasy world.

Sometimes she crept up into the attic to play. It was dark and smelled of tar paper, and she imagined that a host of dangers lurked in the nooks and crannies there. She could hear footsteps creaking on the floorboards behind her and see strange shapes grow into wild animals.

Judy was a very imaginative child. Her dolls had personalities of their own, and they acted out parts in Judy's stories. Her earliest stories were simply imitations of what she saw her parents do, but as she grew older, their plots grew more complex. Everything around her found its way into one of them. The family situations she observed became high drama. She made up adventure stories, mysteries, and romances, like those she listened to on the radio.

When Judy was growing up in the 1940s, kids listened to the radio as much as they watch TV today. As Judy and her brother David ate supper, they listened to the adventures of "Jack Armstrong, the All American Boy." Jack fought pirates in the South Seas and set off through Africa in search of the legendary elephants' graveyard.

On Sunday evenings the whole family sat in the living room and listened to "The Shadow," a suspense show. "Who knows what evil . . . lllurks . . . in the hearts of men?" asked the announcer in a mysterious voice. Then he paused and laughed eerily. "The Shadow knows!"

"You're scared of your *own* shadow," David would tease his little sister. He was four years older than Judy, and he loved to scare her. He would put a sheet over his head and wave his long, thin arms. "Oooooooh," he hooted like an owl. Judy knew who it was, but she would scream and hide under the covers all the same.

Judy was too young to know what real dangers were raging beyond her safe and quiet neighborhood. While she played with her dolls, David played soldier, mimicking the men in combat whom he saw on posters and in the newsreels at the movies. There was a war on. Judy's parents explained that the war was being fought far, far away, and they were safe in New Jersey. World War II, however, had an impact on everyone's life.

Judy's mother and grandmother were constantly knitting scarves and sweaters for the "boys in action." The sweaters were a drab olive color, and Judy thought they were awfully big for boys.

During the war, Dr. Sussman volunteered as an air-raid warden. He wore a white helmet when he went on patrol. David practiced plane spotting in the backyard. He pointed at every plane that he saw, and he could identify several kinds, but they were all American.

One night a siren sounded over the whole city. Judy's mother turned out the lights and pulled down all the shades in the house. She told David to sleep in Judy's room. Mrs. Sussman sat by their beds in the darkness. She told them that the blackout was just practice so that they would know what to do if an enemy plane ever did fly over Elizabeth.

To Judy, the war was like the adventure stories she heard on the radio. The newsreels and war movies made it seem glamorous, full of danger and romance. Whenever the newsreels showed Hitler or Mussolini or Hirohito on the screen, everyone hissed and booed. When the U.S. Marines appeared, the audience cheered wildly.

Judy's memories of the war years would blur over time, but she remembers when it ended in 1945. The Sussmans were spending their vacation at a boarding house in Bradley Beach.

Judy sat in the kitchen in her bathing suit eating a jelly sandwich. Her mother and grandmother were listening to Bing Crosby on the radio. Suddenly his singing stopped. "We interrupt this program to bring you a bulletin from our newsroom," the announcer said. "The war is over. I repeat, the war is over."

Judy's mother and grandmother looked at each other in amazement. "Thank God!" they cried. "It's over at last!" They danced around the kitchen, laughing and crying. The other guests in the boardinghouse joined them, dancing and shouting at the top of their lungs.

That night everyone poured out of the hotels and boardinghouses and marched on the boardwalk that stretched along the beach. Judy's father lifted her onto his shoulders and gave her a horn to toot.

"Can I have your helmet when we get home, Dad?" said David, who was waving an American flag.

"Sure, son."

Judy asked her father why he wouldn't be needing his helmet anymore.

Now that the war was over, he explained, there would be no more blackouts. He wouldn't have to patrol the streets at night. And the boys in action would be coming home, her mother added.

As Judy drifted off to sleep that night, she could still hear the sounds of the celebration . . . cheering and laughing and singing. She didn't really understand what the excitement was all about, but she knew it would make a good story.

Chapter 2

Secret Dreams

After the war, life went on as usual. Every day Judy walked two blocks to school with her best friend, Barry, who lived four houses down from her. One morning, Judy knocked on Barry's door. "Is Barry ready?" she asked.

"Barry's very sick," said his grandmother. "He's not going to school today. He has green tongue."

"Green tongue!" Judy was shocked. She had never heard of that disease. Oh, she thought, what if it's catching!

When Judy got home from school, her mother told her what had happened: "Barry's had appendicitis. He's in the hospital."

Judy never knew if she had just imagined Barry's grandmother saying "green tongue," or if his tongue actually did look green because he was sick. But appendicitis sounded just as bad. Barry was Judy's first friend to go to the hospital. She sent him lots of get well cards.

When Barry returned from the hospital, Judy would stop and see him on her way home from school. He sat on the front porch bundled in a blanket. Judy was afraid to go near him at first because she thought appendicitis might be catching, too.

For a month, Judy had to walk to school alone. Judy enjoyed school. She wore red loafers and thick white socks like all the other girls in her class. To everyone around her, Judy Sussman appeared to be a timid little girl with curly brown hair and wide, dark eyes. But inside, she was a very different person. If she read a Nancy Drew mystery, Judy dreamed she was an ace detective called in by the chief of police to solve a murder mystery. "If I saw a movie about a prizefighter," she remembers, "I was prizefighting my way home." Her greatest fantasy was to become a movie star. After she'd seen Margaret O'Brien in *The Unfinished Dance,* she pictured herself as a ballerina in pink satin toe slippers. She was waiting patiently for a Hollywood producer to discover her.

Judy told no one about her secret dreams except her father. Of all the people in her family, Judy was closest to him. "He always encouraged me to catch the moon." If Judy wanted to be a movie star, her father said, why not? Rudolph Sussman was a dreamer like his daughter.

Judy's father had thick black hair, a black mustache, and a twinkle in his eye. He was fun-loving and playful.

Judy and her father laughed together and shared jokes that weren't funny to anyone else. They played lots of secret games, but their favorite was hide and seek. As soon as Judy heard her father's car in the driveway, she put her shoes in the middle of the floor and ran away to hide. Dr. Sussman could tell where she was hiding by which way the toes of the shoes were pointed. Sometimes Judy pointed the shoes in the wrong direction just to fool him.

Judy liked visiting her father at his dental office. When she went to get her teeth checked and cleaned, Miss Fay, her father's secretary, would let her sit at the typewriter. Judy pecked at the keys while she waited for her appointment.

Judy called her father Doey-Bird or Doey for short. That was her special nickname for him; nobody else called him that. Just before she got into bed every night, Judy would shout, "Ready for the treatment, Doey!" After her father had tucked her in, Judy would give him his treatment—a sliding kiss up one cheek, across his forehead, and down the other cheek, three quick hugs, and a butterfly kiss on the nose.

Doey was always there when she needed him. He took her temperature when she was sick. He sat in the bathroom with her when she had stomach cramps and shampooed her hair when she had a scalp infection.

Judy remembers her parents' wedding picture. Her mother was beautiful—tall and slender with blond hair and creamy white skin. Mrs. Sussman was a quiet person. Unlike her husband, who joked and played with his children, and sometimes lost his temper, she kept her feelings to herself. Although she worried about everyday problems, to Judy she seemed very calm in times of trouble.

When Judy came home from school, she usually found her mother reading. "My mother always, always had a book," Judy remembers. The house was filled with books. Volumes and volumes lined the bookshelves on either side of the fireplace in the living room. There were books in the bedroom, and books on shelves in the sun parlor.

Mrs. Sussman was a great library-goer as well. While her mother browsed in the adult section of the library, Judy went to the children's room. She loved being surrounded by books. She even liked the way they felt and smelled. Old books smelled dank and musty. New books had a different smell. She liked to sniff the perfume of fresh printer's ink, and thumb their white, crisp pages.

Judy's favorite book when she was small was Ludwig Bemelman's *Madeleine*, which she read over and over again. One day an overdue notice came in the mail for *Madeleine*. "Where is it?" Judy's mother asked. "I don't know," she said.

Notices came for several months and every time her mother asked, Judy shook her head. She never told her mother that she had stashed the book in the bottom drawer in the kitchen where she kept her playthings.

Judy's favorite aunt, Aunt Francis, whom she called Fanta, also loved books. Fanta was like a second mother to her because she didn't have any children of her own. She would hold Judy in her lap and read out loud to her. Fanta was a grade school principal and the only person Judy knew who owned more books than her mother. Her books were kept in perfect order on polished shelves: illustrated storybooks, leather-bound novels, cloth-covered classics. Fanta handled her books with great care. They were so beautiful that Judy could hold them only if her hands were clean. Someday, Judy thought, she would have a fine collection of books like that.

Fanta and Uncle Herb lived in an apartment across town, so Judy visited them often. Almost all of Judy's relatives lived in Elizabeth: Uncle Eddie, who was a dentist like Doey, Uncle Philip, Uncle Bernie, Grandma Sussman, and Nanny Mama.

Judy's grandmother, Nanny Mama, had a grand piano at her house. Uncle Bernie used to play while the family crowded around to sing. When Judy was alone, she would sit at the piano, pressing the keys and making her own music. She spent hours pretending to play in Uncle Bernie's grand style.

Aunt Gert was one of the few relatives who did not live in Elizabeth. She had an apartment in New York City, and on holidays—Thanksgiving and Passover—Judy and her family took the train into Manhattan to see her. Aunt Gert's apartment was very elegant. When Judy took a nap there, she slept amid lace pillows on her aunt's chaise lounge. Beside it was a glass-topped table covered with dainty little jars and tiny snuffboxes. Once Judy stayed overnight at Aunt Gert's by herself. The next day they rode a double-decker bus and shopped at Macy's.

The Sussmans were a happy family, but they shared sad times, too. Grandma Sussman died when

Judy was ten years old. Then Aunt Anna died. Judy was not allowed to go to their funerals because she was too young. But afterwards, relatives and friends gathered at the Sussmans to "sit shivah" for a week. Judy was there for that.

When a Jewish person died, it was the custom for relatives and friends to help the family through their time of mourning by sitting shivah. They brought baskets of fruit and homemade cookies. The house was full of people who talked about the loved one who had died and remembered the happy times they'd had together.

To Judy, sitting shivah was like a big party, but she dreaded the unveiling ceremony that was held a year after every funeral. The grave of a dead person was marked by a carved footstone. At unveilings the footstone was covered with a white cloth, and then removed.

The ceremony was very emotional. After the rabbi said a prayer, the cloth was pulled away. When the footstone was uncovered, everyone felt the shock of losing their loved one all over again. It frightened Judy. No one explained the meaning of what was happening, and she was afraid to ask.

Judy was a sensitive child who felt things deeply. As she grew older, feelings and fears collided inside of her in great confusion. What was it like to die? she wondered. What did it feel like to lose someone you loved very much?

The adult world was exciting and scary, too. Its forbidden secrets loomed beyond her grasp like a distant dream. She tried to imagine what it would be like to be grown up.

She searched for books that would give her the answers, but all that she could find were Nancy Drew mysteries, biographies, and books about girls who loved horses. Where were the books about real kids with real feelings? Judy wanted to read a book about herself—about her desires and fears and wild imaginings.

Chapter 3

A Big Adventure

"I'll miss you, Doey-bird." Judy was curled up on her father's lap. She turned away, biting her lip to keep from crying.

"And I'll miss you." Doey was fighting tears, too.

Judy still could not believe that she was going to spend the third grade in Miami Beach, Florida. Miami was more than a thousand miles away. It took a whole day and a half to get there by train.

Judy was awestruck when her parents announced that they had rented an apartment in Miami Beach for the winter. It was the best thing, they assured her. Judy's brother, David, had been sick with a kidney infection, and he needed to be in a warm climate to get better. It would be good for Judy, too, her mother said, because she wouldn't get as many sore throats through the winter.

Everyone was going—Judy and David, their mother, and grandmother Nanny Mama. Everyone except Doey, who could not leave his dental practice in New Jersey. He promised to visit them at Thanksgiving and Hanukkah.

Judy couldn't stop worrying about Doey. After all, this was his bad year. Uncle Abe and Uncle Eddie had both died when they were forty-two years old. Doey was forty-two, and Judy was convinced that something terrible was going to happen to him just like his older brothers.

She felt better when she found out that Fanta and Uncle Herb were making arrangements to rent their apartment and move into Judy's house to keep Doey company. Still, she wished that she could take care of him herself.

Judy's parents decided it would be best to leave for Florida in October. That would be late enough to avoid the hurricane season in Miami but still early enough for Judy and David to start school. At the end of September, Judy invited some friends home for a farewell lunch, and then she said good-bye to her classmates and teachers. Even though Judy tried to think of her trip to Miami as a big adventure, it would not be easy to switch schools and make new friends.

On a Saturday morning, the Sussmans all went down to the train station in Newark. Doey went on board the train with them for one last good-bye. Then he joined Fanta and Uncle Herb, who were waiting on the platform. Judy waved and blew kisses as the train pulled away.

Their train was called the East Coast Champion. The seats on the Champion were soft and comfortable, not hard like the seats on the train to New York City. Judy laid her head back against the plush cushion and lost herself in a Nancy Drew mystery.

Time passed quickly on the train. Judy and David walked to the club car; they played cards and drank Cokes. At night the porter showed them how to tilt their seats back so they could go to sleep. When the Champion pulled into Richmond, Virginia, the conductor announced that all black passengers had to go to the back of the train.

"Why?" Judy asked.

Her mother explained that in the South black people didn't ride with whites.

"That isn't fair," Judy protested.

"No, it's not," her mother said.

Judy didn't understand segregation—the separation of white and black people. It was the first of many things that were new to her. She wanted to ask why people practiced segregation if it wasn't fair, but she had the feeling that her question wouldn't be answered.

So Judy settled back and went to sleep. When she woke up the next morning, she was in Florida. "Jacksonville," called the conductor. Judy was surprised to see that everything was still green. In New Jersey the autumn leaves were turning red and yellow now.

As the day wore on, Judy watched the scenery change from pine forests to palms. It seemed forever before the conductor called, "Next stop, Miami, Florida."

Judy's adventure was about to begin. As soon as they got off the train, the Sussmans took a taxi to their new apartment in Miami Beach. They drove past

a long line of luxury hotels with glamorous names—
the Shelbourne, Roney Plaza, the Versailles—to the
apartment district.

The taxi stopped at a pink stucco building with a
goldfish pool in the front. The apartment was not at
all what Judy had expected. It was ugly and bare
without curtains and rugs.

To make matters worse, it was very, very small.
Judy and David didn't even have bedrooms; they
would have to sleep on couches in the living room. At
home Judy had her own bedroom with twin beds so
that friends could stay with her overnight.

So far Judy hated Miami Beach. When she went to
bed that night, she could hardly sleep. She missed her
bedroom in New Jersey and her friends. Most of all,
she wished that Doey was there to tuck her in.

The next day Judy's mother took her to school.
Central Beach Elementary School was a long, low
building with a red tile roof. It covered one whole
block. Judy was used to a small school. At home she
had had the same kids in her class since kindergarten,
and she knew all the teachers. This school was so big!

At first Judy was shy and quiet, but little by little
she began to make friends. Peter Hornick, the boy
who sat behind her in class, began to tease her.
Sheila, Linda, and Shelby, three girls who lived in the
same apartment building, asked her to play with
them. Soon the four girls were together all the time.

There was something to spending the winter in
Florida, after all. For one thing, there was so much to
do outdoors. Judy and her friends played hopscotch,

rode their bicycles to Flamingo Park, and swam at the beach. Their mothers let them stay out until it got dark. Not only was it warmer and sunnier than in New Jersey, but even the days seemed longer.

After Christmas vacation, Judy and Sheila Rosenberg started ballet lessons once a week. Judy had taken ballet ever since she was three years old. She loved to dance, especially for an audience. One day she decided to stage a ballet show for the people in her apartment building. She directed the show, designed the dances, arranged for the costumes, and made the programs. She and her friends spent days practicing their dance steps at the beach.

Judy had put the show together, and she wanted to do the whole program with "Starring Judy Sussman with Added Attractions." The other girls wouldn't let Judy get away with that! They wanted all of their names to be included as stars.

The ballet show was a big success. After the performance, the girls passed around a glass jar and collected ten dollars for Hadassah, their mothers' favorite charity.

Thirty years later when Judy wrote a book about her adventures in Miami Beach, she called it *Starring Sally J. Freedman as Herself*. Most of the things that happened to Sally really happened to Judy, including the contest to try on Margaret O'Brien's pink satin toe slippers.

A local shoe store had invited all the ballet students in Miami to try on the ballet shoes that Margaret O'Brien had worn in her movie, *The Unfinished*

Dance. Whoever fit into the shoes would win the contest and get a free trip to Hollywood for a screen test and lunch with Margaret O'Brien herself. This was Judy's chance to be discovered as a movie star. She described the big moment in *Starring Sally J. Freedman as Herself:*

Sally knew exactly how Cinderella must have felt when it was her turn to try on the glass slipper. . . . She took off her sandal and held out her foot, digging her fingernails into the upholstered arms of the chair. The shoe man held out Margaret's pink slipper. It didn't have a boxed toe, like Sally's toe shoe. This toe was covered with satin, like a professional ballerina's. She eased her foot into the shoe. It fit! She didn't have to bend her toes or anything. Her whole foot went in easily. She smiled. But, wait . . . there was too much space *around* her foot. Maybe the shoe man wouldn't notice . . . .

"Sorry, sweetheart . . ." the shoe man said to Sally. "It's too wide for your narrow little foot." . . .

She felt like crying. . . . If she did her voice would break and then nothing would stop the tears.

Judy didn't win the Margaret O'Brien contest, but it was exciting all the same. Everything in Miami Beach was exciting. There were so many things you could do in Miami that you couldn't do in New Jersey.

When Judy's mother took her to the movies on

Friday and Saturday nights, they always went out afterwards for a chocolate sundae with lots of hot fudge and mounds of whipped cream. Nothing in New Jersey could compare with those sundaes. On New Year's Eve, the Sussmans went to the Orange Bowl Parade to watch the marching bands and floats. Judy dreamed of twirling a baton in the parade some day.

The best thing about Miami was the beach. The water was warm and clear, and the sun was always shining. At Bradley Beach on the Jersey Shore, where Judy usually spent her summer vacations, the ocean was cold and the waves were so high that she could not go very far from shore.

The Sussmans lived within walking distance of the Fifteenth Street beach in Miami. On Saturdays they would pack a picnic lunch and spend the afternoon at the beach. Sometimes the Rosenbergs went along. Judy and Sheila practiced cartwheels on the beach and collected seashells while their mothers talked.

Mrs. Sussman never went near the water because when she was a little girl her father had thrown her into the ocean at Atlantic City to teach her how to swim. She had nearly drowned, and she never tried to swim again. Nanny Mama enjoyed the ocean, but she didn't swim, either. She would stand at the water's edge and splash herself just enough to get wet. Then she would walk back up the beach and sit on a beach chair with Mrs. Sussman and Mrs. Rosenberg.

Judy loved the ocean, especially bobbing on the waves in her big black inner tube. She spent hours just floating, gazing at the blue sky and daydreaming.

"I used to picture myself as Esther Williams," Judy remembers, "swimming underwater without getting water up my nose."

Judy knew she would never learn to swim that way if she didn't try. So she decided to teach herself to swim. David teased Judy when he saw her trying to swim by moving her arms and kicking one foot. "You're not really swimming," he would say with a laugh. "You've got one foot on the bottom." She did keep one foot on the bottom, but that was how she learned to swim—by pretending. One day she could lift both feet from the bottom and kick while she was actually floating.

When Judy's father came down to Miami during the holidays, he took David and Judy to the beach. They built elaborate sandcastles and played games in the water.

On his trip down for David's thirteenth birthday, he asked the children if they wanted to take a ride in the *Goodyear Blimp*. Kids were fascinated by the blimp that hovered over Miami Beach. It was always there, like the palm trees and glimmer of the ocean. Judy loved to watch the silver bubble, but she wasn't so sure that she wanted to ride in it.

The passengers were loaded into a little compartment on the underside of the blimp. As it started to rise silently in the air, Judy's stomach turned a somersault and her hands got sweaty. She wondered what it would be like to die. But when the huge airship began to glide effortlessly through the sky, Judy forgot her fright and gazed down at the hotels that looked like little match boxes standing on end. Doey glanced across at her and smiled. She smiled back.

Judy felt good. She had tried something new and a little scary. She should stop worrying and learn to enjoy new experiences. Riding in the blimp *was* exciting, much more fun than watching it from the ground. As the blimp started its descent, Judy realized that if she had not come to Miami, she never would have felt the thrill of riding in the *Goodyear Blimp*.

Soon she would be going back to New Jersey. Miami's stucco buildings and tropical trees no longer seemed strange. She felt at home here. She could barely remember her first day at Central Beach Elementary School when she had run home crying. From now on, Judy knew it would be easier for her to make new friends. Perhaps she was becoming more adventurous.

When the Sussmans were ready to go back to New Jersey in June, Judy's father drove down so that they could have plenty of time to sightsee on the way home. They were going to visit Saint Augustine and the Bok Tower and historic landmarks that Judy had read about in school.

While Judy was packing her books and toe slippers and Margaret O'Brien paper dolls, a strange thought crossed her mind. She almost forgot! The year was over and her worst fears had not come true—Doey didn't die. She thought that she might never see him again, never hear his laughter, never crawl up into his lap and give him a treatment. She was glad that he was now forty-three.

A photo album of Judy as a child and her family. This is her baby picture, taken with her brother David when she was six months old.

Judy's parents, Esther and
Rudolph Sussman, as they
looked when Judy was a baby.

Vacation. Two-year-old Judy
takes a stroll on the boardwalk
at Bradley Beach.

A couple of years later, Judy dresses up for a formal portrait.

A visit to Atlantic City. In back of Judy and David stands Nanny Mama with her three children: Judy's mother, Fanta, and Uncle Bernie.

Judy cuddles with her mother.

Florida! Judy takes a mystery story to the beach.

Florida is lush and green in the wintertime. It's warm enough for Judy to put on her pretty peasant blouse, and David wears shorts.

(**Left**) *This is the outfit Judy wears to do cartwheels at the beach.* (**Below**) *The lifeboat David and Judy are sitting on is used to rescue people in danger of drowning.* (**Facing page**) *Judy strikes a ballet pose in front of the junior-senior high school in Miami Beach.*

Fun at the beach has a special excitement when Doey comes down to visit.

When she's floating free in her inner tube, Judy can be anyone she'd like to be, even Esther Williams. Move over, Esther!

Ready for takeoff. Judy takes a ride in the Goodyear Blimp.

Chapter 4

Almost a Woman

Judy gazed at the basement in awe. Doey had hinted that a surprise was waiting for her at home, but she had no idea that it would be so wonderful. A new rec room, paneled in pine with green vinyl built-in seats to match the green and black tiles on the floor. As soon as it was finished, Doey promised, they would have a party.

But Judy would have to wait one more year before her father finished his special project. The Sussmans had decided to rent the apartment in Miami Beach again. Judy left New Jersey in October as she did before; she went to school in Florida and returned in June. This time when she came back, the recreation room was ready for a party.

Her parents agreed that Judy could invite boys to her first party. She had invited girl friends for lunch and slumber parties, but she had never had a *real* party with boys as well as girls.

On Saturday morning everyone was busy at the Sussmans. Judy and her parents set up a table and chairs in the basement while David planned games for the party that night. Every time Judy passed a mirror, she glanced at her fluffy short hair. She would have a new look for the party. Her mother had set her hair in pin curls the night before to make it come out right. Without her pigtails and ribbons, Judy felt much older.

At four o'clock the doorbell rang. As Judy's friends arrived, Mrs. Sussman met them at the front door and took them downstairs to the rec room. When they were all seated at the table, she served them sauerkraut and hot dogs.

Doey took home movies. Sammy thought that Dr. Sussman was taking snapshots. He posed for the camera by dangling a fork full of sauerkraut in front of his mouth for the longest time. When the movies came out, there was Sammy, grinning with his mouth full of sauerkraut and sitting very still while everyone around him was talking and eating.

Judy's brother, David, was in charge of the entertainment. He had built carnival booths and thought up lots of different games. One of the things he made was a chubby little green man who held a bunch of brightly colored balloons. Everyone had to take a balloon and prick it with a pin. Inside each balloon was a piece of paper that told the kids what to do: "Turn around a hundred times . . . make a funny face." The balloon game was the hit of the party.

Judy liked having parties at her house. On Friday nights her girl friends would bring their sleeping bags and spend the night, talking and listening to records. One of their great delights was filling the bathtub with bubblebath. Then they would all crowd in and cover themselves with suds.

Once Judy and her friend Rozzy filled the tub with a whole box of soap flakes when Dr. and Mrs. Sussman had gone out to dinner. The bubbles were extra thick and there were thousands of them. When the girls let the water out, the tub was still filled with suds. Judy and Rozzy looked at each other, wondering what to do.

They scooped up armfuls of suds and tried to flush them down the toilet. They flushed and flushed, but the bubbles kept fizzing up. Soapsuds spilled out of the toilet and covered the floor. Judy and Rozzy finally gave up. They tiptoed to bed, hoping that somehow the suds would disappear by morning.

When Judy's parents came home that night, they heard a funny sizzling sound coming from the bathroom. They turned on the light and couldn't believe their eyes. There were soapsuds everywhere: piled high in the tub, all over the floor, even in the sink!

In the sixth grade, Judy belonged to a secret club. All of her best friends were in the club—Rozzy, Ronne, Nancy, and Anne. They called themselves the Pre-Teen Kittens, and they met after school at each other's houses. Sipping Cokes and munching Oreos, they would sit on the porch and talk about the boys they liked best.

Each of them kept a list of their favorite boyfriends on the back of their desk blotters at school. They compared lists frequently and discovered that everyone liked the same boys.

One afternoon after school, the PTKs ganged up on a boy named Michael. "We all came after Michael and he ran, but he was no match for us. When we caught him, we held him on the ground and took turns kissing him. And he just cried and cried and cried. It was *not* fun for him."

Judy and her friends were also intrigued with the physical changes going on in their bodies. Menstruation was a mystery and discussed at great length. What did it feel like to get your period? Who would get it first? Who would be last?

Judy had been thinking about that for a long time. When she was nine, she had visited her relatives on Long Island. Her cousin, who was several years older, could not play that day because she said she was sick. "What's wrong with you?" Judy asked. "You'll find out when you're thirteen," was all that her cousin would say.

On the way home in the car Judy asked her parents, "What will I find out when I'm thirteen?" That night Doey put Judy on his lap and tried to explain menstruation. Judy's first sex talk left her with more questions than answers. "My father told me that it had to do with the lunar cycle that occurred *every* twenty-eight days, so I thought whenever the moon was full, women all over the world were menstruating."

Rozzy had a book about menstruation which her mother had given her. The girls studied it together, puzzling over drawings of ovaries and fallopian tubes that only confused them more.

Judy was disappointed. Books seemed to deal with sex in such an abstract way; they never talked about feelings. Judy wanted desperately to know what it felt like to have your period. Was it painful? Did everyone know when you were having your period? Did you feel more grown up?

Judy's friends began to get their periods. First Rozzy, then Anne. Judy tried not to show her feelings, but she was jealous. What if she was the last one to get it? What if she never got it at all?

"I wanted my period so badly," Judy says today, "that I once put a pin in my finger to draw blood. I smeared it on a pad and wore the pad just to see what it felt like."

"You're too impatient," said her mother. "Girls don't begin to menstruate at the same age." She tried to comfort Judy by telling her that she didn't get her period until she was sixteen. That only made Judy feel worse.

Judy was as eager to look like a woman as she was to have her first period. She noticed with despair that she was more flat chested than her friends. Small boned, her mother said. Just be patient, she was told. But Judy didn't want to wait.

She bought her first bra with a friend on a shopping spree downtown. Both girls squeezed into a tiny dressing room no bigger than a closet. They each tried on bras until they found ones that fit. Judy's was a plain white double-A padded bra.

When she got home, she rushed upstairs, closed her bedroom door, and took off her clothes. Then she put the bra on and looked at herself in the mirror. Her bra would look so nice with a little help. She did the same thing that she would have Margaret Simon do in a book she wrote years later, *Are You There God? It's Me, Margaret.*

I went into the bathroom and opened the bottom cabinet. There was a whole box of cotton balls. *Sterile until opened,* the package said. I reached in and grabbed a few. My heart was pounding, which seemed stupid because what was I so afraid of anyway? I mean, if my mother saw me grab some cotton balls she wouldn't say anything. I use them all the time—to put calamine on my summer mosquito bites—to clean off cuts and bruises—to put on my face lotion at night. But my heart kept pounding anyway, because I knew what I was going to do with the cotton balls.

I tiptoed back to my room and closed the door. I stepped into my closet and stood in one corner. I shoved three cotton balls into each side of my bra. Well, so what if it was cheating! Probably other girls did it too. I'd look a lot better, wouldn't I? So why not!

I came out of the closet and got back up on my chair. This time when I turned sideways I looked like I'd grown. I liked it!

Judy could get her period any day now, and then she would begin to grow for sure. She was almost a woman.

Chapter 5

Together Yet Alone

Judy's friends were very special to her. They had played together on roller skates and bikes. Together they had bought their first bras, shared their secrets, and whispered their worries about growing up. Junior high school, they knew, was going to bring changes to their friendship. At Hamilton Junior High they would be meeting kids from other grade schools and changing classes. No longer would the five girls— Judy, Rozzy, Ronne, Anne, and Nancy—be in the same room and have the same teachers. And as their birthdays came in the seventh grade, one by one they would become teenagers.

As it turned out, being thirteen was special. Judy made new friends in junior high, and many of them were Jewish. At that age the boys were being bar mitzvahed—a Jewish ritual that celebrates the coming of manhood on a boy's thirteenth birthday. The religious service in the synagogue was followed by a big celebration at a hotel.

"There was one formal affair after another," Judy remembers. "We were all invited. It went on all year—

Barry's this week and David's next week."

The bar mitzvah receptions were very elaborate. Long tables glittered with stemmed glasses, silver, and flowers. The food was fabulous. After dinner the lights were dimmed, and a big birthday cake was rolled in. Proud relatives and friends stood around the boy who was being bar mitzvahed as he blew out the candles. A photographer snapped their picture, and everyone clapped.

The seventh-grade boys had to wear jackets and ties to bar mitzvahs, and the girls wore long party gowns. Judy and her mother had gone into New York on the train one Saturday to shop for Judy's first formal party dress.

Along with the gown, she bought her first pair of nylon stockings and a garter belt and fancy bra. The garter belt and bra were made of blue lace to match her blue net gown. Her party shoes were silver with small wedged heels to make her a bit taller.

The girls wore the same dresses to all the parties. Judy's lasted almost the whole year, but there was still one bar mitzvah to go when a boy accidentally stepped on the net and tore it. A net overskirt is hard to mend without the rip showing, but somehow Mrs. Sussman fixed it so that no one noticed it. "There was never any question about wearing that gown for the last party," Judy says. "You got one long party dress, and that was it!"

In junior high, Judy and her friends continued to have parties in their recreation rooms, but the parties had changed. Instead of balloon games, they played kissing games. The boys suddenly became as interested in kissing as the girls.

Judy was first kissed by a boy while they were playing post office. Everyone had to pick a name out of a hat. Then each girl went into another room with the boy whose name she drew.

Judy picked Pat Flannery's name. Her friends smiled. Every girl there wanted to draw his name, and Judy had been lucky enough to get it.

She started giggling the minute she was alone with him.

"If you don't stop laughing, how am I supposed to kiss you?" he said.

Her stomach turned over. "He's going to kiss me on the lips," Judy thought.

And he did. It was a quickie, but it was her first real kiss.

Judy's house became the most popular house for parties. All the kids had record players in their rec rooms, but Judy's was the only one with a juke box. A patient of her father's was in the business, and he had gotten it for the Sussmans.

The kids also liked to gather around the grand piano in the Sussman's living room and sing popular songs. Judy enjoyed sitting down at the piano and playing for her friends.

She remembered how surprised she had been when her father had bought the secondhand piano after her first trip to Florida. She was thrilled and couldn't wait to take lessons.

She had always wanted to play piano like her Uncle

Bernie. When she did start lessons, she was disappointed because the teacher only showed her how to play with one hand. *Putt, putt, putt* . . . Her teacher smiled. "That's right, dear. Just like the little steamboat." Judy sighed. How could she ever learn to play like Uncle Bernie by doing that!

Over the years, she had gotten better, and now she played quite well. Playing at parties, with everyone looking over her shoulder and singing along, was fun.

Judy was trying all sorts of new things. In the eighth grade she switched music teachers so that she could learn how to play the pop songs that added such life to her parties. Her parents encouraged her and said that she could take any class that interested her. She was learning to paint and draw and weave. In her illustration class Judy and her friend Zelda were designing dresses. They decided they would become fashion designers when they were older.

Judy's father taught her to appreciate fine music by playing his records for her in the evenings. After dinner, she and her father would sit alone in the sun parlor and listen to the great composers. Doey had built a bookcase that held a small record player and his collection of albums, which were kept in perfect order.

Their evenings in the sun parlor were quiet, intimate times between Judy and her father. They never talked about the music; they just listened in silence. Once in a while he did talk with her, though, about his way of looking at life. Dr. Sussman was a reader of philosophy. Later, when Judy was in college and took philosophy herself, she recognized the names of thinkers he had mentioned years before. Judy wished they could have more of those talks. On her own she was discovering adult books by writers like Ayn Rand and J.D. Salinger.

As Judy became more aware of how her body was changing, she was also becoming more aware of her feelings. She had always been very sensitive. When she was little, her mother once said, "We never have to punish Judy. All we have to do is look at her the wrong way and she'll cry." She had shared her secret feelings with her parents then. They knew how frightened she was of the dark and dogs and thunderstorms. But by the time she was ten, she began to keep such things to herself.

Judy was no longer as close to her family as she once had been. She was the only child at home now that David had left. He had graduated from high school and was going to Penn State. Sometimes she almost wished he was there to tease her now and again.

Although she still laughed and joked with her father, and she loved to listen to his records, she no longer shared her private concerns with him. And she could not confide in her mother.

Instead, Judy told her mother what she wanted to hear, especially about parties, dances, and dates. If Mrs. Sussman asked her if she had a good time, Judy always answered yes. For her mother's sake, Judy wanted to be the prettiest, most popular, best-dressed girl in her class.

Sometimes the party was miserable. Then Judy wished she could tell her mother the truth. "I had a terrible time. Nobody asked me to dance. I hated the whole thing!"

The growing distance that separated Judy from her parents seemed to widen every time she said what they wanted to hear instead of what she really thought. When Judy was hurting inside and pretending to be happy, the pain seemed magnified because she suffered it alone.

She tried to please her parents and to be a perfect daughter. She got As in school, and she was never in trouble. "I was a good girl," she remembers. "That was my role in life. Perhaps it was because my brother was a rebel. He kicked his kindergarten teacher in the stomach."

Secretly, Judy wished that she could be more rebellious. Why couldn't she do exactly what she wanted and say just what she felt instead of trying to act so perfect? Even as a little girl, Judy had felt a thrill when she did something she knew her parents would not approve of. "It was delirious, wonderful."

Judy needed to share her real self with someone who could understand. Someone who would not condemn her for wayward thoughts as her parents and teachers might. Someone who would take her seriously. All of her girl friends seemed too interested in boys and football games to talk about anything else. Or were they just pretending, too? It occurred to her that the worst thing about being a teenager was feeling completely alone.

Chapter 6

Summers Away

"Judy." Her mother's voice sounded faint and far away. Judy was spending the summer at Stockbridge Work Camp when she got the call from home. She was startled to get a phone call so late at night. Something terrible must have happened.

"What is it?" Judy's heart stopped. She felt the tears coming even before her mother said—

"It's Nanny Mama. She died two hours ago."

Judy dropped the phone. The words caught in her throat, and then she started to cry. She had known that her grandmother was very sick. Nanny had moved in with the Sussmans when she could no longer take care of herself. A few months ago, she had gone to the hospital because her cancer was getting worse. Even though her parents did not discuss it openly, Judy knew that Nanny was dying.

Still, Judy could not believe that she would never see her grandmother again. There was an empty feeling in the pit of her stomach.

With tears streaking down her cheeks, Judy ran out into the night. She wanted to be alone. She sat on her favorite rock beside the lake and gazed into the darkness for a long time. She thought of all the good times she had had with Nanny: playing the piano at her house as a little girl, watching Nanny in her purple-flowered bathing suit splash in the shallows when they had gone to the beach. Nanny was so good, so kind.

Judy always had a warm, loving feeling when she thought of her grandmother. She could not put into words why she felt that way, but somehow she knew that she could do no wrong in Nanny's eyes. Nanny would love her no matter what.

Judy could not stop crying. Even though she had sat shivah many times for her relatives, the pain of losing someone she deeply loved had not yet touched her. She had barely known her aunts and uncles who died. Even Grandma Sussman was a stranger.

Judy was ten when Grandma Sussman, her father's mother, died. Judy had whispered in his ear, "I'm sorry." Her father simply said, "Grandma is no more." That was the only explanation Judy had ever had of death.

Now at fifteen, Judy knew that Nanny was gone forever. But what did that mean? Maybe her parents hadn't told her because they didn't know.

Judy talked to her mother on the phone the next day. Mrs. Sussman didn't want Judy to come home for the funeral. She wanted her to remember Nanny the way she had been. Judy was relieved. In some strange way, thinking of her grandmother laughing on the beach eased her pain.

Years later Judy would write about Nanny's death in a book called *Forever*. The main character, Katherine Danziger, is a teenager who receives a phone call at camp, telling her that her grandfather has died. Like Judy, Katherine is bewildered and angry as she begins to realize that life and love do not last forever.

Summer camp was an important part of Judy's life. She liked spending summers away from home. For eight weeks she was free and had to answer to no one. Likewise, there was no one to turn to in case of trouble. She had to learn to cope with problems on her own.

Judy started to go to sleep-away camp when she was eleven. For four years she went to a girls' camp in Connecticut. Every June her mother would pack a trunk load of shorts and polo shirts, and Judy would board the train for Camp Kenwood.

Camp Kenwood was on a lakeshore surrounded by pine trees. The campers slept in cabins on bunk beds, and each girl was responsible for keeping her own bunk tidy. Every hour of the day was filled with something to do. If the girls weren't playing volleyball or softball, they were out on the tennis courts. They were big on singing, too. "We sang everywhere we went, in the dining room before meals and at night before we went to bed," Judy says.

It was at Camp Kenwood that Judy finally learned to swim. In Miami she had taught herself to stay afloat and tread water, but she had never really learned to swim the right way, with her face under the water.

She had always been afraid of getting water up her nose.

But at camp she had to learn the right way. She didn't want to spend every summer as a red cap! The beginning swimmers had to wear red bathing caps and stay in the shallow end of the lake. This area was called the Crib because it was surrounded by a narrow walk where the counselors stood and watched the beginners. Each counselor carried a bamboo stick just in case someone needed to be pulled out of the water.

After her first summer at camp Judy took her blue cap test. The middle swimmers were allowed to swim outside the Crib where the water was over their heads. To pass the blue cap test, the girls had to swim four laps between two ropes.

The distance was about forty feet, but on the day of the test it looked like forty miles to Judy. She didn't think she could ever do it. One by one, her friends jumped in and earned their blue caps. Judy's stomach was jumping up and down. What if she drowned? What if she was the only twelve-year-old who had never passed the test?

"Judy Sussman." The counselor looked up from her clipboard. "Ready?"

Judy nodded.

"One, two, three," the counselor counted. "Jump!"

Before she knew it, Judy was in the water, kicking her feet and blowing bubbles out of the side of her mouth. She could hear the counselors rooting for her.

"Go, Judy. Go!"

She did all right until the last lap when she started to get tired. She could hardly lift her arms, and her legs felt as heavy as lead.

"Don't stop now!" shouted the counselors. "You can make it!"

Just when Judy thought she would sink to the bottom of the lake and never be seen again, her hand touched the rope.

Everyone cheered. She had done it! Judy was limp and every muscle in her body ached, but it didn't matter. She felt the thrill of accomplishing something that she never thought she could do. It was a wonderful feeling.

The next summer Judy passed her white cap test and became an advanced swimmer. The white caps could swim anywhere, even out to the raft. And they never had to take a swimming test again. What a relief!

Judy's most memorable experience at Camp Kenwood would always be the day she passed her blue cap swimming test. She would write about the fear and triumph of that day in her book, *Otherwise Known as Sheila the Great.*

Judy's camp experiences weren't all as much fun. When she was fifteen, she went to Stockbridge Work Camp, a summer she wished she could forget. Everything that could go wrong, did. The final blow was the phone call from her mother telling her that Nanny had died.

At Stockbridge, boys and girls worked together on different projects. They built a stone bridge, put up a bathhouse on the lake, and turned an old barn into a theater.

Judy was working on the theater crew when she broke out in a rash. She had been painting the foundation poles with creosote, and her hands and arms were covered with bumps from an allergic reaction to the chemical. At first the camp nurse thought Judy's rash was poison ivy so she coated her arms with calamine lotion. When she found out that it was an allergy, the nurse decided to wrap Judy's arms in bandages. She looked like a mummy!

As soon as the bandages came off, Judy was playing baseball when a fly ball smashed into her face. She had a bump on her nose for the rest of the summer.

But looking a little funny didn't bother her nearly as much as the loneliness. Judy felt more grown up than many of the fifteen-year-olds, and yet she was not sophisticated enough to hang out with the older crowd of kids. She just didn't fit in, and she made few friends.

Her good friend, Rozzy, who had come with her to Stockbridge, became part of the "in" crowd. That made Judy feel even more alone. Judy had always had lots of friends; she had never been left out before.

She thought of Mara, a girl who had been in her cabin at Camp Kenwood one summer. While Judy was having a good time with her friends, she gave Mara only a passing glance. Mara was an outsider. The kids weren't cruel to her, but they weren't kind either. She must have had a terrible time.

Now Judy was the outsider. Deep down inside, Judy knew it didn't matter if she wasn't part of the "in" group, but it hurt all the same. As long as kids hung around in groups, someone would always be on the outside.

When Judy came home from Stockbridge, she did not tell her parents how miserable her summer had been.

"Did you have a good time?" her mother asked.

"Great!" said Judy, putting her shorts and polo shirts away. What else could she say?

Every time that Judy returned from her summers away, she felt like a different person. She had always changed in some way. The painful memories of Stockbridge were as much a part of her as the good times at Camp Kenwood. After she passed her blue cap swimming test, she had gained greater confidence. When she faced her grandmother's death alone, she felt a deeper pain than she had ever felt before. How could she explain those things to her mother? She didn't understand them herself.

Chapter 7

Friends

Judy remembers her high school days not so much for the classes and teachers as for the kids who were her friends. Battin High School was big. There were about twelve hundred students at the time Judy went there. She wonders now about the friendly, easy atmosphere and whether it had anything to do with the fact that the students were all girls.

"There was no such thing as sexism at our school," Judy says. "We ran the show. The paper, the yearbook, the clubs, the politics." And Judy Sussman was in the thick of things. She worked on the newspaper for two years, sang in the chorus, and went in for modern dance, besides. She may not have been able to fill Margaret O'Brien's toe shoes when she was a little girl, but in her senior year she danced well enough to make the performing dance troupe.

Her best friend was still Mary Sullivan. All through junior high they had sat next to each other in homeroom: first Sullivan, then Sussman. Judy and Mary looked like sisters. They were both slender and about the same height with dark brown, shoulder-length hair. Judy thought Mary was prettier, with her blue eyes and turned-up nose. Often they wore matching skirts and sweaters with little white collars.

Mary spent so much time at the Sussmans that she was almost one of the family. She and Judy had a fine time together, and if Mary was sometimes as troubled as Judy was, she didn't let it show. "As close as we were," Judy says, "she didn't confide in me about the kind of things that she might have been going through. I didn't either. Everybody kept up an outside appearance as if everything was wonderful."

Both girls loved the theater. They went into New York to see the latest plays and imagined their own names in lights some day. "We really fancied ourselves as very fine actresses," Judy remembers.

All through the tenth grade, Judy and Mary tried out for parts in school plays. Finally, they were given one-liner walk-on parts in a play called *Stage Door*. It was about a group of young women living in New York, who were trying to become actresses.

One afternoon when the girls were rehearsing, Phyllis Kirk, a well-known actress, strolled into the auditorium and sat down. Judy couldn't believe her eyes. She had never seen anyone as glamorous as Phyllis Kirk in her charcoal gray suit and chartreuse picture hat.

After the rehearsal Miss Kirk chatted with the aspiring young actresses. She told them that she was a graduate of Battin High. When she was their age, she had been in *Stage Door*, too. Phyllis Kirk had acted in the same play on the very same stage!

As the famous actress walked out of the auditorium, the girls studied her every movement. Miss Kirk wore a long, sleek page boy and bangs. The girls noticed the way she threw her head back to flip her long hair out of her face. It was her trademark. For weeks afterwards they threw their heads back in just the same way.

Phyllis Kirk's mother was a nurse at the hospital where Judy and Mary worked as volunteers after school. The girls were waitresses in the coffee shop, and when they saw Mrs. Kirk sit down, they fought over which one of them would get to take her order.

Judy and Mary were part of a larger group of friends who hung around together at Battin High. Still others were fun to work with in chorus, modern dance, and the newspaper. For the first time Judy had black friends, too. Both blacks and whites were in the dance group, and the girls laughed and joked and goofed off together. To Judy, who had been so puzzled by segregation in the South, it felt healthy, good.

Lunchtime, when everybody got together after their separate classes, was one of the high points of Judy's day. It was crowded and noisy, and even today Judy can remember the mingled smells of the brown-bag lunches. "Oh, nothing tasted so good as those lunches!" she says. Her mother usually made a sandwich like tunafish or peanut butter and tucked in a brownie or cupcake for dessert. Every day Judy bought two cartons of milk, stuck a straw in each, and drank them at the same time.

After school the girls often got together at Pamel's, a soda shop in downtown Elizabeth. The waitresses weren't especially glad to see them, and there was one who really didn't like them. They left her tip in the bottom of a milkshake glass, just as Tony Miglione and his friends did in *Then Again, Maybe I Won't.*

When Judy was a sophomore, there was a series of parties as the girls turned sixteen. Since Judy's birthday was February 12, hers was the first.

The Sussmans spent days decorating the rec room for her Sweet Sixteen party. Her father blew up dozens of pink balloons and sprayed them with silver sparkles while her mother tied sugar cubes to pink ribbons that hung from the ceiling. On party day the entire basement ceiling was covered with balloons and sugar cubes. Judy's friends all dressed up and brought dates. First, they had a formal sit-down dinner in the dining room and then went downstairs to dance.

It was a special evening for Judy, and she invited a special boy she had met at Christmas. Bernie was a young man really, since he was four years older than she and a sophomore in college. He was handsome, with dark, curly hair. Bernie looked older than the other boys she knew and acted older, too. Judy was a little frightened of him and attracted to him at the same time. Bernie seemed to know how she felt. He didn't try to push her into something she wasn't ready for, but they went to movies and parties together on and off for six years.

There were other boys in Judy's life besides Bernie. "I was usually in love," says Judy. When she was a junior, she went steady and wore her boyfriend's class ring on a chain around her neck. Like her other romances, that didn't last long. Judy fell in and out of love regularly.

Mary and she talked on the phone for hours about their boyfriends. One time they even liked the same boy. He would take Mary out one night and Judy out the next. After Mary had a date with him, Judy would call her and ask, "How many times did he kiss you?" Mary would call the next night: "How many times did he kiss *you?*"

Judy and her friends did not discuss sex openly, as they had when they were in the sixth grade. They whispered about girls who were known to play around, but they kept their own sexual experiences a secret.

Once Judy overheard a girl boasting that she had been out with Bernie, listening to the radio in his car, till two in the morning. Bernie didn't have a car radio. Judy knew exactly what that meant, and she was very jealous.

Even so, Judy was not about to let her feelings get the best of her, with Bernie or anyone else. Her mother had told her that there were two kinds of girls: those who let boys have their way and those who didn't. Nice girls saved sex for marriage. It was an unwritten law that boys liked to have sex with girls who were willing, but they married the girls who refused them.

Although Judy had car dates since she was in the ninth grade, she didn't park with boys. Her parents believed it was dangerous for two kids to be alone in a car where they could be attacked or robbed so easily. Judy could stay up as late as she wanted to, as long as she told her parents when she got home. She and her date spent their time in the sun parlor where her father and she had listened to records.

Judy brought her dates home, but she admits that she tried parking just once. She and her date drove up to Orange Reservation where it was woodsy and quiet. No sooner had they pulled off the road when another car came up beside them. Suddenly, a police officer was looking down at them and asking,

"What are you doing?"

"Nothing. *Nothing!*"

"How old are you?" he asked Judy. "Would you like me to call your parents? Would you like your parents to be told about this?"

Of course, she didn't! That was the end of Judy's parking experiment, and she didn't even have time to get kissed.

For the girls at Battin High, boys were people to have fun with on weekends. During the week Judy was buried in a busy round of studies and school activities. It was at Battin that she first tested her writing skills. She was recommended for the journalism class by her ninth grade English teacher, and that is how she came to be on the newspaper. Judy's journalism teacher, Mr. Komishane, was also her creative writing teacher during her junior year. He was tall, slender, and very good humored, with a wonderfully silly laugh. Judy wrote the words and music to several ballads that she sang aloud to the class. One was about a wagon train going west:

Oh, once there was a boy
And he did love a girl,
Yet old fate had different plans
For they were goin' to different lands.

Why is life so cruel?
Why are people so afraid?
They were a-headin' Westward,
Watch out for an Indian raid.

"Profound? No!" as Judy herself says. "But my ballads were great hits, and Mr. Komishane recorded them. How I'd love to hear them now!"

As a senior, Judy was busier than ever. After two years as a reporter on the newspaper, she was named feature editor. She shared the editorship with Mary. Together they dreamed up story ideas and assigned them to kids in the sophomore journalism class, who were now the reporters. Her favorite was called "People Resemble Animals."

By now Judy was good enough to make the modern dance performing troupe, and she brought a special touch to rehearsals. Her own sound effects, in fact. As she glided gracefully across the stage in her blue leotards and bare feet, the other girls never failed to giggle. It wasn't that Judy was a bad dancer—it was her noisy toes. She could bend her toes back and forth to make them snap just as other people could crack their knuckles. Unfortunately, her toes snapped on their own when she didn't want them to. During the hush of a performance they seemed even louder. Her toes would make their funny cracking and popping sounds, and Judy could hear her friends muffle their laughter off stage.

In her senior history class, Judy felt for the first time what it might be like to be a college student. Her history teacher, Dr. Strohl, addressed her as Miss Sussman. It sounded very dignified. Judy worked for weeks on her term paper, which required careful research. She picked the topic, "Should the United States Adopt the Metric System?" because she had heard her father and his friends discussing it.

Dr. Strohl encouraged his students to think about the issues that affected their lives every day. They talked about politics, current events, world problems—subjects that didn't have easy answers. They had to look at both sides of the argument and back up their opinions with good reasons.

Judy was a good student. It never occurred to her not to do her homework or to go to class unprepared. She and Mary sat together in the last row in their senior zoology class, and they were usually in trouble. Mary was the one who was blamed most often for talking and carrying on, but Judy admits that she had more than a little to do with the uproar in the back row. Just once Judy decided not to study for a zoology test. She wanted to prove to herself that she could fail a test and live through it. Her carefree attitude changed as soon as she started to take the test. She knew that she didn't remember enough to pass it. "It wasn't so much fun when the test came back with an *F*."

Judy and Mary missed their senior prom. They went instead to June Week at the Naval Academy in Annapolis, Maryland, with a couple of cadets whom Mary had met. The week was filled with parties, dances, and parades. Judy and Mary had a great time, not with their dates, but with each other. They were hysterical the whole week, full of laughter. They loved being together for one last fling. One crazy rainy day they raced through the campus, giggling and getting soaked.

June Week was the first time that Judy came up against religious prejudice. Her date hadn't known she was Jewish, and when he found out, he became cold and standoffish. Judy watched the change come over him, and she grew very, very angry. "It was a real shock," she says, "that anyone of my age could possibly feel that way."

A week later Judy and Mary were sitting side by side in white caps and gowns at their own graduation ceremony. As the principal called the names of the graduates, the two girls clutched each other's hands. They were nervous, happy, and frightened all at the same time.

After high school, Judy and Mary would go their separate ways, but they promised always to be friends. Mary was accepted at the American Academy of Dramatic Arts to study acting. Judy planned to attend Boston University to get a degree in elementary education.

Judy graduated with high honors. At the top of her class, she could have gone anywhere to college. She picked Boston University for no special reason except that a friend had told her, "That's where the boys are."

Chapter 8

A Death in the Family

In September, Judy's parents drove her up to Boston and settled her in Charlesgate Hall. Judy's dormitory room, which she shared with two other freshmen, was barely big enough to hold three beds, three small chests of drawers, and three desks. There was one closet for the three of them. The girls had all come to school with trunks and suitcases, and by the end of the first day they were sending home half of it with their parents.

Boys were the last thing on Judy's mind as she said good-bye to Dr. and Mrs. Sussman. She was very tired and felt thoroughly dragged out from a headache she had had for the past week. Still, she didn't tell her parents on the chance that they might not let her stay at college. In the days that followed, she felt no better. Orientation week was hectic, confusing, and exciting. Though her head was throbbing, Judy threw herself into the activities just as she had at Battin High.

The freshmen were scheduled to leave for a three-day trip to a campsite for orientation meetings. But before they left, each student had to go through a thorough medical examination.

Judy wondered if she should tell the doctors that she'd been having headaches, that she felt tired all the time, that she couldn't eat, but she decided she'd better not. It was probably just the excitement that made her dizzy. And if there really was something wrong with her, the doctors would find it. Judy was relieved when they said she was fine.

The day before the freshmen were to leave for their trip, Judy felt so sick that she couldn't make it through the day. She collapsed in her dorm room; and her roommates had to take her to the infirmary in a taxi. The nurses shrugged their shoulders—another case of homesickness. As Judy's fever rose higher, they became concerned. A series of tests showed that she had mononucleosis.

Mono. Kids called it the "kissing disease" because it was a virus that passed from mouth to mouth. When someone came down with mono, everyone knew why. Judy thought that hers was due to a summer romance with a boy named Michael.

College officials phoned the Sussmans and told them their daughter was very ill. She would have to be sent home. Judy was so sick that she had to be carried to the plane on a stretcher.

For more than a month, she lay in bed, staring at the ceiling like a zombie. How could her first semester in college begin with such promise and end so miserably? She was back where she'd started: her mother's baby, needing to be cared for day and night.

After missing weeks of classes, Judy couldn't go back to school that fall. She would have to start again in the spring. When she was strong enough, she took a part-time job typing and filing. Occasionally, one of her friends would stop by to visit and tell her about college life. Judy felt her own life had been suspended.

In the spring Judy decided to go to New York University instead of Boston. "I never want to see Boston again," she told her parents. She wanted to make a new start somewhere else. She also felt safer being close to her doctor and her family in case she had a relapse.

New York University was located in the heart of Manhattan in Greenwich Village—one of the most exciting parts of the city. The Village was crowded with college students browsing through paperback bookstores, listening to poetry readings and folk music in coffeehouses, and playing chess in Washington Square. They wore long hair, beards and beads, and baggy black turtlenecks.

Judy wore a loose black turtleneck and olive green corduroy jeans like everyone else. She and her friends drifted in and out of art galleries, sidewalk cafés, and bars. "We walked around the Village and pretended to be very Bohemian," she remembers.

For Judy, being a beatnik was play acting. She enjoyed the role of an intellectual college student, independent and carefree, rebelling against society. It was fun to be different. But when she went home, she left her baggy turtleneck and jeans behind and slipped back into her skirts and sweater sets.

The Sussmans had moved from Elizabeth to West-field, New Jersey. During Christmas vacation of her sophomore year, Judy was invited to a party at a house around the corner from her parents. The boy who invited her was a law student at New York University. There were other law students at the party, but Judy was attracted to one of their friends who had already graduated from law school, John Blume. "I remember icy blue eyes," Judy says, "and I liked him a lot."

John was twenty-five. Judy listened intently as he told her about his work in the judge advocate's office at Fort Dix. After he got out of the army, he planned to join his father's law firm in Newark. He knew exactly what he wanted to do with his life; he had mapped out every step of the way. Judy was impressed.

Judy fell in love again, but unlike her high school romances, this one lasted. She dated John through the spring and summer. They went to plays and ate dinner in intimate, candlelit restaurants. It was not long before Judy was dreaming of marriage and children and living happily ever after.

John, however, was not sure that he wanted to get married. After ten months of steady dating, he needed time to think. He told Judy that he wanted to stop seeing her for a while. He promised to call after a month and tell her how he felt.

The month passed slowly for Judy. Finally, John called. He said he wanted to come over and talk. They went for a late night walk. The December air was brisk and chilly. Huddling close in the cold, John told Judy that he loved her. She said yes when he asked her to marry him.

John seemed to have a streak of good luck. In his brother-in-law's poker game he won enough money to buy an engagement ring. The next day he took Judy to look for a ring. She was surprised when they walked into a garage instead of a jewelry store. John explained that he had a friend in the tire business who could get diamond rings wholesale. Judy didn't ask questions. She just wanted to wear John's ring.

John's friend was busy changing tires when they found him. He put his tools down and shook hands with John as he congratulated the happy couple. Then he slipped behind a glass counter that was filled with automobile accessories. He pulled out a little black square of velvet and placed it on the counter. Inside the velvet were three diamond rings. "You can have whichever one you want," said John.

Judy was so excited that she could hardly make up her mind. After trying them all on, she settled on a ring with an emerald cut blue-white diamond. The ring was too big for her finger, but John's friend said he could send it back to the jeweler to be adjusted.

"Oh, no. Absolutely not." Judy didn't want to let the ring out of her sight. So she wore it even though a piece of tape had to be wrapped around it so it wouldn't fall off.

The wedding was scheduled for August. There were so many things to do before then. Judy had to choose her china and crystal and silver. Invitations had to be mailed, and the catering arranged. It was going to be a big wedding with ninety people at the Hampshire House in New York.

Judy's brother David flew home especially for the wedding. For four years he had been stationed in Libya with the Air Force. On a beautiful summer afternoon in 1959, Judy drove with her parents to pick up David at Newark Airport. He strolled off the plane looking tall and handsome in his uniform, with his wife beside him. They all were in high spirits and bubbling with conversation.

On the way home, David announced that he was going to become a father. Judy's father got so excited that he almost drove off the road. His only daughter was getting married, and now a grandchild was on the way. "What a year for the Sussmans!" he said, grinning from ear to ear.

Everyone piled out of the car. David brought the luggage in while Judy's mother showed her daughter-in-law around the new house. Judy was the only one who noticed her father lie down on the sofa as soon as he walked into the house. She asked if he was all right. Sure, he said, he just felt a little strange. But after an hour when he still didn't get up, Judy called the rescue squad.

As they waited, Judy knelt beside the couch and held her father's hand. "This is the wrong time," he said, barely above a whisper. Her father died before the rescue squad could get him to the hospital. Judy heard his last desperate breaths. There was nothing she or anyone else could do to save him.

Her father's sudden death from a heart attack at age fifty-four made Judy realize what a fragile thing life really was. Only hours before, he had been full of fun and laughter. "What a year for the Sussmans!" he had said, looking forward to the wedding and the prospect of grandchildren. When he died, part of Judy died, too. She was no longer a child. For a long time now there had been no hide-and-seek games and special kisses. Now she said good-bye, too, to that warm, safe feeling she had had so many years ago when she snuggled in her father's arms. She was grown up now. Soon she would be a woman with a family of her own.

Judy grows up. Her first times spent living apart from her family were at summer camp. Here she is at thirteen with Nancy Bloom, her favorite counselor at Camp Kenwood.

Judy with her friends from Camp Kenwood **(facing page and above)** and Battin High **(below)**. She's at the foot of the bed in the top photo and in the center of the last row in the bottom photo.

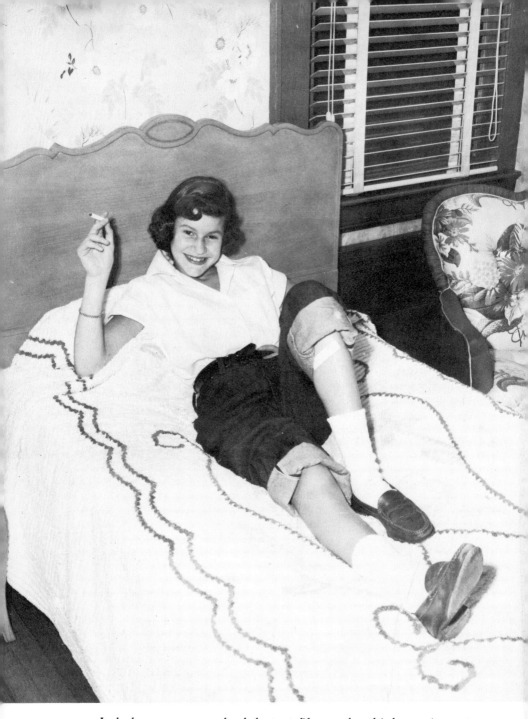

Judy has never smoked, but at fifteen she thinks a cigarette makes her look sophisticated for the camera.

(Above) *Judy's best friend in high school visits her in 1962, when they both have daughters of their own. Mary Sullivan, now Mrs. Weaver, looks on while Judy gives Anne* (left) *and Randy* (right) *a hobby horse ride.*

(Left) *Judy in 1966 with her children, Larry and Randy. Randy is wearing a mortarboard and holding a diploma because she's graduating from nursery school.*

Judy at home in Santa Fe. **(Above)** A TV crew films her at the typewriter. **(Left)** Judy's mother, Judy, and sixteen-year-old Larry in the summer of 1979. **(Facing page)** One whole wall of Judy's living room is lined with books.

A best-selling author promoting her books. In New York Judy poses with Alex Santo, a cardboard character from Superfudge **(above)** and signs copies of the book in a crowded Toronto bookstore **(below)**.

*Back in Santa Fe, Judy drops in on Larry in the record store
where he works.*

Judy today in the desert near her home.

Chapter 9

Something of Her Own

Judy married John Blume in a small ceremony at the Sussmans' home. The lavish affair at the Hampshire House had been cancelled, but the wedding still had to take place as planned. According to Jewish custom, a wedding must not be cancelled because of death, even if it occurs on the same day.

The first year of marriage wasn't easy for Judy. She felt torn between loyalty to her new husband and guilt for not spending more time with her mother. She knew that her father believed that life is for the living, but what about her mother? Mrs. Sussman never talked about her husband's death—about what the loss meant to her, about how her life had changed. John, too, never talked with her about that sort of thing, and she was afraid to tell him about her mixed feelings.

By the time Judy graduated from NYU, she was pregnant with her first child. She had planned to teach second grade, but now her teaching career would have to wait. Judy's daughter, Randy, was born in 1961.

After Randy was born, the Blumes moved to a new garden apartment in Plainfield, New Jersey, closer to John's law office. The apartment had five rooms, and Judy filled them with beautiful furniture and a forest of plants.

Two years later the Blumes moved to a house in Scotch Plains where Judy's son, Larry, was born. Larry slept in the nursery now, and Randy had a room of her own with the same bedroom furniture that Judy had used as a little girl.

Judy was happy and busy taking care of her family. They lived on Winding Brook Way in a suburban ranch-style house. "It was a street of other people like us," Judy remembers, "young families and a lot of children."

Judy's life as a homemaker and mother soon settled into a comfortable routine. She took care of the house in the mornings, and in the afternoons there was time for reading and needlework while she watched the children play in the backyard.

At twenty-five, Judy had everything she thought she wanted: a husband, two children, and a house in the suburbs. But after a few years the idea of marriage, which had once seemed so glamorous, was no longer exciting. Judy began to realize there was an empty spot in her life.

She had loved music, dance, and art as a child, but the routine of a young mother gave her no such outlet for her creativity. After Randy and Larry started nursery school, she thought about getting a job.

But doing what? She had a degree in elementary education, and yet she was far from sure that she wanted to teach. Teaching had been more her mother's idea than hers. She remembered Mrs. Sussman's advice: go to college to get a degree in education in case, God forbid, you should have to work. As a teacher you can always get a job. Judy knew she needed something else in her life, something of her own. Just once, she wanted to please herself— not her mother, or John, or the children.

Her first try at a career was song writing, but she gave up when she realized that her songs were only imitations of records she heard on the radio. Then she tried making colorful felt banners for children's rooms. She sold her first order to Bloomingdale's department store in New York City. For a year she sat in her basement, glueing felt pictures together, until she became allergic to the glue. Her fingers started peeling, and she had to do something else.

That's when she thought of writing children's books. Randy was five now and Larry was three, and Judy was reading picture books to them. While washing the dinner dishes, she would make up rhyming stories that sounded like the ones she read to her kids. She illustrated her stories with colored pencils and sent them to publishers. Week after week, they were sent back.

"The first rejection slip sent me for a loop," says Judy. She hid in her closet and cried. Gradually, she hardened herself until she could accept six rejection slips in a week. She would go to bed praying, "Please let me be published. I don't even care if they pay me. Just let me be published."

Judy was about to give up and try something else when she received a brochure in the mail from NYU. It listed classes available for graduates and she noticed one called, "Writing for Children and Teenagers." She decided to take it.

Monday nights became the highlight of her week. John would take the children out to eat on Mondays while Judy rode into New York on the bus to take her class. Before class Judy always ate supper at the Cookery in Greenwich Village. She ordered a hamburger and salad just as she had done as a college student years ago.

It felt good to be back in the Village. Judy watched the long-haired girls walk by in their jeans. Marriage and motherhood were the last things on their minds. All the options were still open to them: they could have careers and get married later or not at all. Judy envied their freedom.

After dinner, Judy melted into the crowd of college students and went to her writing class. She loved being with other people who shared her interest in writing. No one mentioned Scotch Plains or the PTA or the weekend golf game. They talked about writing.

Lee Wyndham, who had published several children's books, gave lectures on preparing manuscripts, writing cover letters, and getting agents. Occasionally, guest speakers—editors and publishers—talked to the class. Judy was fascinated by the world of publishing. She wanted to know more and more.

Every week the class turned in manuscripts for their professor to criticize. Mrs. Wyndham was impressed by Judy's writing. "She wrote me little notes telling me I would get published one day," Judy recalls. Judy knew that no one could teach her how to write, but she needed professional encouragement. When the course was over, she decided to take it again.

She went to the library daily and came home with armloads of books. She divided them into two groups. "These are the books that I really like—I enjoy reading them. I would like to write books like these." And in the second pile, "These are the books that bore me and probably are boring to children, too. I don't want to write like this."

John was glad that Judy had finally found something she enjoyed doing. He would smile when he found her pounding away on her old typewriter on the kitchen table. Still, Judy had the feeling that he didn't really take her writing seriously. Writing was becoming more and more important to her. It hurt her when she heard John tell his friends, "All I have to do is buy Judy some paper and pencils and she's happy!"

After two and a half years of rejection slips, Judy started getting checks in the mail. She published two short stories, "The Flying Munchkins" and "The Ooh-ooh-aah Bird." Then *Trailblazer* magazine ran *Iggie's House* as a serial.

In 1969, Judy received a phone call from Reilly & Lee. They wanted to publish what would be her first book, *The One in the Middle is the Green Kangaroo.*

"I was overjoyed, hysterical, unbelieving!" says Judy. Randy and Larry were playing in the basement with their friends. When Judy grabbed a handful of their papier-mâché and threw it up in the air, Larry's best friend, Laurie Murphy, ran home and told her mother, "Larry's mother is crazy!"

A few days later the mailman, Ernie Powell, came walking up the driveway with a check for $350. Time after time, he had glumly delivered rejected manuscripts; now he was grinning. Judy and Ernie danced across the front lawn.

As soon as Judy's book was published, a newspaper reporter and photographer arrived on her doorstep. Her picture appeared in the *Westfield Leader* the next day with an article headlined, "Mom Keeps Busy Writing Books for Little Children."

She sent a copy of the book to Randy's third grade class, and Randy's classmates sent Judy cards telling her how much they enjoyed it. "I felt like such a celebrity," Judy remembers.

Pride in what she had done was something that John seemed unable to share. He wasn't unhappy about her writing, but he saw it strictly in terms of earning money for doing a job. After all, Judy had gotten nothing for years of writing, and rewriting, and being turned down, before she was finally published. What she was getting now didn't seem worth the effort. He didn't understand that to Judy it wasn't the money. It was so much more.

Chapter 10

Not Just Pretend

Judy drove along Route 80 to Englewood Cliffs, New Jersey. She was looking forward eagerly to her appointment with Mr. Jackson. Then the huge complex of glass and steel that was the publishing house of Prentice-Hall loomed in front of her. Her eagerness turned to terror. "All you have to do is find the parking lot and we'll find you," the editor had said.

Somehow Judy found the receptionist. She was told that Mr. Jackson would be with her in a few minutes. Judy collapsed in a chair, waiting. She took a pill to settle her stomach, but she was still nervous. Mailing off manuscripts to an editor was one thing, but meeting one in person now seemed terrifying.

Judy had read in *Writer's Digest* magazine that Bradbury Press was interested in realistic fiction for young people, so she had sent them a draft of *Iggie's House*. They didn't accept the manuscript or reject it. Instead, they asked if she would meet them to talk about it.

"Hi, I'm Dick Jackson." She looked up at the young man with a wide grin. "You must be Judy."

She nodded. The stomach pill made her mouth so dry that she could barely talk. Dick Jackson smiled, trying to put her at ease.

They walked down a long corridor that seemed to go on forever. Judy felt like a little girl again, walking down the long corridor of Central Beach Elementary School to Miss Davis's third grade class. No matter how old you are, she realized, there are always "firsts" in your life that are very exciting and very frightening.

Dick led her to a tiny office that was littered with manuscripts, stacked on his desk and piled high on the floor. He explained that Bradbury Press was a year old. There were only two editors, he and his partner. Although their offices were located within the massive headquarters of Prentice-Hall, someday they hoped to move out on their own.

Then he turned his attention to *Iggie's House*. Judy's first novel was about a black family who moves into an all-white neighborhood. Winnie, a girl down the street, becomes their friend even though the neighbors don't approve. Prejudice was a topic that deeply interested Judy. She believed that whites and blacks could be friends if they lived together.

Dick Jackson liked the manuscript and with some revision, he said, it might work out as a book. Maybe, he added cautiously. "Now," he said, leaning back in his chair, "what do we know about Winnie? What kind of person is she?" For an hour and a half, Dick asked Judy questions about her characters, about the plot, about where the book was going.

Judy took notes furiously. New ideas began to spin out of her imagination. They talked about tightening scenes, cutting chapters, and adding new dialogue in places. By the end of the meeting, they were both exhausted.

Her work had only begun. Dick said that he could not offer her a contract yet. If she was willing to revise the manuscript, making the changes they had agreed on, Bradbury would consider publishing it. Maybe.

For a month Judy worked on her story so hard that it seemed as if she never left her typewriter. When she had done all that she could, she sent the new version back to Dick. He called with the great news that Bradbury had accepted the book for publication.

This time when Judy went back to Bradbury, Dick and his partner, Bob Verrone, took her out to lunch. They were very excited about publishing *Iggie's House*. Judy was exactly the kind of new talent they were looking for. She had shown herself to be an author who was open to new ideas and one who was willing to revise to produce the very best book possible.

Over lunch Judy mentioned that she had already started working on another book. It was very different from *Iggie's House*, which she had done as homework for her NYU writing class. "That was written by me," she said, "but it wasn't me writing as me."

Judy wanted to write a book from her own experience, about what it felt like to be a twelve-year-old growing up with lots of questions. She could remember everything about that age: how she talked to God about her private problems and how embarrassed she was because she was the last of her friends to start menstruating.

No one had ever dared to write about religion and sex from a kid's point of view. Judy was proposing to do something that had never been done before. The two editors, however, believed in Judy's idea. "We were utterly disarmed," Dick says. "She was young and we were young. It was appealing from the start." Kids talked about those subjects everyday. Why shouldn't they be able to read about them in books?

Judy didn't consider what she was doing as daring. It was just honest. She had always wanted to write the kind of book that she would have enjoyed reading when she was twelve—a book about real kids with real feelings. Now she had the chance.

Judy went home and completed the first draft of *Are You There God? It's Me, Margaret.* in only six weeks. It flowed out naturally: she simply wrote down exactly what was on her mind when she was in the sixth grade. "In *Margaret*," Judy says, "I just let go and wrote what I wanted to write and told the truth about what I felt."

By the time she finished *Margaret, Iggie's House* had already been published. The reviewers criticized her first novel for being too simplistic. Judy admitted that it was not very good, but the words of the sharp-tongued reviewers hurt. "It was very painful," she remembers. "If I hadn't already finished another book, I don't know if I could have gone on."

When *Margaret* was published, Judy prepared herself for the worst. Whatever the critics said about this book, she was proud of it. Her other two books were the work of a beginner. *Margaret* was the first book that she had written straight from her heart in her own way.

One day as Judy was dashing out the door to play tennis, Dick Jackson called. He had received an early copy of the *New York Times Book Review*, and he wanted to read their review of *Margaret*. "A warm, funny and loving book," Dick quoted with pride, "one that captures the essence of adolescence." Then he told her that the *Times* had named *Margaret* as one of the outstanding children's books of 1970.

Judy was jubilant. She was so excited that she sang in the car and hummed as she went through the grocery store that afternoon. She remembers that day as a high point of her career. "That was the first I felt, 'I really can do this! These people are taking me seriously! It's not just pretend.'"

Critics praised the book for its honesty and freshness. They were impressed by the way Judy told the story in the first person, as if Margaret were telling her own story and sharing her deepest concerns.

Not everybody liked *Margaret*. Judy gave three copies of the book to Randy's and Larry's elementary school, but they never appeared on the library shelf. The principal wouldn't allow them because the books dealt with menstruation. Schools in other cities also banned the book. "I was angry beyond words," says Judy.

Even though some school officials and parents tried to keep *Margaret* out of libraries, kids read it anyway. As soon as the paperback came out, they bought copies and shared it with their friends. Dick Jackson says that the overwhelming popularity of the book was due to this "underground kid-to-kid fever."

Then the fan mail started. Hundreds of kids across the country sent letters to Judy. "You don't know me but you wrote this book about me, and I *am* Margaret," said a twelve-year-old girl. "You know just how I feel," wrote a thirteen-year-old. "It's like you're still a kid."

Margaret's success was a turning point for Judy. She began to think of herself as a professional writer. After she finished one book she was hard at work on another, and in a few short years she had written half a dozen novels.

Now when she visited Dick Jackson, she traveled to Bradbury's new offices in Scarsdale, New York. Instead of leisurely restaurant lunches, they ate sandwiches in Dick's office while they worked. They were both very busy and successful. Bradbury was a thriving company, and Judy Blume had become a best-selling author. "How did this ever happen to me?" she asked Dick.

Judy was invited to speak at writers' conferences and book association meetings. People thought of her as a leader in her field because she had broken away from the usual style of children's fiction and used a new style of her own. "I don't care about rules and regulations of writing for children," she told her audiences. "They say you mustn't write in the first person; they say you must never leave loose ends. I said I was going to do it my way anyway."

Her books raised more questions than answers, but life was like that, said Judy. There weren't always neat endings. Her stories explored the problems of growing up and described the emotions kids really feel—joy, fear, loneliness, and uncertainty. They made kids laugh and cry because they were true.

Many of Judy's ideas came from her own family and friends in Scotch Plains. When she wrote *Blubber*, a story about a fat girl who is tormented by her classmates, some critics said that kids could never be that cruel. But the book was based on an experience in Randy's fifth grade class. Every night Randy would come home and tell her mother how the kids in her class were teasing a particular girl. One day when the teacher left the room, the kids locked the girl up in a closet and put her on trial.

Judy decided to write a book about a teenager who suffered from curvature of the spine because she knew a girl in the neighborhood who had scoliosis. In order to write *Deenie*, Judy watched kids being fitted for body braces in the hospital. "My favorite scene in the book," she says, "is the scene in the plaster-room. All of that dialogue is real. I sat there with a pencil and paper and wrote down everything the nurse and doctor said. The children were very frightened and said nothing basically."

When Randy was thirteen, she asked her mother to write a realistic teenage love story. In *Forever,*

Michael and Katherine promise always to be true to each other. But as they grow older, they become different people and their relationship changes. Finally, they decide to go their separate ways.

In real life, Judy was discovering the same thing. She had vowed to love her husband forever, but she was becoming a very different person from the girl he had married. Her writing career allowed her to grow in ways she had never dreamed possible. To keep growing, she needed new challenges and change.

At first she thought that a new house might provide that change she needed. After living nine years in Scotch Plains, the Blumes moved to Martinsville, New Jersey, where they bought a beautiful home with a swimming pool tucked away in the woods. But Judy still wasn't happy.

Her life with John had always been safe and comfortable. "It was a nice marriage," says Judy, "but inside I was dying." During the spring of 1975 Judy and John separated. She moved to Princeton, New Jersey, with Randy and Larry. It was not easy to explain to them why their mother and father had decided to live apart.

Only two years before, Judy had written a novel, *It's Not the End of the World,* about a girl who learns to cope with her parents' divorce. "When a marriage is about to dissolve," she says, "the children want to know why and they have a right to know. They're thinking, 'How is this going to mess up my life?' "

Judy decided to put her feelings in a letter which she gave to each of her children. "They went to their rooms to read it because they needed to be alone," she remembers. "Then we all got together and cried."

The following fall was the most difficult time in Judy's life. She was lonely, frightened, depressed. Judy had been raised to be a wife, and now she found that she didn't know how to be an unmarried woman. It was a hard time for Randy and Larry, too. While the divorce was not the end of the world, it brought a time of mourning and a time of pain.

A few months earlier Judy had met Tom Kitchens, a physicist, and they had become friends. When Tom took a job in London, England, he and Judy stayed in touch by writing letters. Tom was divorced, too. Like Judy he was lonely and felt uprooted. Both of them were eager to find love again, and it was not long before letters were not enough. Judy and her children moved to London for six months, and in May 1976 Judy and Tom were married. Shortly afterwards they moved to Los Alamos, New Mexico, where Tom had accepted a job at the atomic laboratory.

It all happened too fast. They hadn't given each other the time to let old wounds heal, and they hadn't taken the time to get to know each other. They were married, Judy now believes, for all the wrong reasons. Although they did their best to make it work, they had too little in common. After three years of trying to build a marriage, Judy and Tom were divorced.

Still, Judy believes strongly in marriage. "But the partners have to be right for each other," she explains. "That means not jumping in and hoping for the best. You can't hope that the other person will turn out to be what you want. Loving means liking and respecting and caring—taking the time and trouble to learn about the other person." Judy feels this way about all the people she's close to—her children and her friends as well.

"I am a loving person," she says, "and I love hard. When you do love that intensely, you open yourself up to be hurt, but it's worth it. You can't be afraid to make mistakes. You can't spend your life saying, 'What if.' "

Chapter 11

Judy Blume as Herself

Dressed in jeans, Judy sits on her living room sofa in Santa Fe, New Mexico. At five foot four and one hundred pounds, she is about the same size as the kids she writes about. Her dark hair is just long enough to swing as she moves, and it frames a face that changes quickly from sadness to joy.

A sense of excitement runs through her conversation like a bright thread. She talks with her whole body, leaning forward as she makes a point, adding exclamation points and question marks with her hands. She looks both young and wise at the same time, and as she talks, she leads you into her world.

Judy divides her time between New York City and Santa Fe, a small town high in the Sangre de Cristo Mountains. When she is in Santa Fe, she lives in a sprawling, one-story adobe house with the rough-cut beams and tile floors typical of the Southwest. Colorful Navajo rugs adorn the walls, and sunlight filters through the long, low rooms. A picture window reveals the mountains beyond. "The scenery is so beautiful, I have to face the wall to work," says Judy.

Judy jogs a mile every morning over the juniper-covered hills near her home. She likes to ski and play tennis. When she goes grocery shopping in her jeans and T-shirt, no one recognizes her or asks for her autograph. It is here that she writes the first drafts of her books.

When she's working on a story, Judy's characters become so real to her that she talks about them at the dinner table as if they were real people.

"Guess what Davey did today?" she says to Randy and Larry.

And her kids will say, "Oh, what did she do today?"

"Well," says Judy, "you won't believe this but . . ."

Judy has always enjoyed sharing her writing with her children. When she was writing *Forever*, Randy would come home from school and rip the paper out of the typewriter to see what happened to Katherine and Michael that day. For the past ten years, Randy has been her mother's first reader. "Sometimes I will tell Mom that no one my age would use those words, or I will hit on something from my own experience that needs to be changed a little," Randy explains. "I can see it better from the kid's point of view."

Randy and Larry can be depended on for honest feedback, even when it hurts. When Judy went on national TV for the first time, she was petrified. According to Randy and Larry, she had acted that way, too. "You looked like you were strapped to the electric chair. You didn't say anything too stupid, but you didn't say anything really good either."

Now Judy has been interviewed on dozens of TV

and radio shows. She's used to the glare of TV lights and the countless questions she is asked every day. When *Wifey,* her adult novel, was published, Judy went on tour for three weeks. "I did a city a day. I flew in at night, went to sleep, and got up in time for the early morning TV talk show. I ran around all day from interview to interview—TV, radio, and newspapers— then flew to the next city that night and went to bed. The next morning I got up at six and started all over again."

When Judy travels across the country, promoting books and giving interviews, she misses being at home. And it's hard work. There are times when it is so tiring that she wonders why she is doing it. Even in Santa Fe, she wishes she had more time to spend with her family. When she is writing a book she spends hours by herself, day after day, alone at her typewriter.

Every working woman, Judy says, has to face the same conflict between a career and family life. Still, she would never go back to her mother's time when women were content to be wives and mothers. "My mother had many, many talents and much to offer. Everyone would have been a lot happier, including my father, if she had worked outside the home."

Judy feels that her work has enriched her family life. Randy, for instance, is keeping all her options open. Whereas Judy grew up with the belief that she would marry and gave little thought to planning a career, her daughter puts these goals in the opposite order. Randy knows that she will have a career. She will marry when and if she chooses to do so.

Judy's career has affected Larry, too. When he was small, he wanted "a milk-and-cookies Mommy." As he grew older, he began to understand that writing was an important part of his mother's life. Now that he is about to go off to college, he has a positive attitude about women, working, and motherhood.

This may have come about because Judy was open about her work and its problems with Randy and Larry when they were young. They also felt free to confide in her. When Judy herself was young, she could not talk openly to her parents about her thoughts and feelings. She decided that when she became a parent, she would try to answer her kids' questions as honestly as she could—even if it was painful at times. She wanted not only to be their mother, but also their friend.

"Kids live in the same world as adults do," says Judy. "They see things and hear things. Problems only get worse when there are secrets, because what kids imagine is usually scarier than the truth."

The same quality of openness that Judy brings to her relationship with her children is found in her books. Each story is told by a child who confides in the reader as if to a best friend. "How do you know all my secrets?" asks one of her fans.

She gets a thousand letters a month from young readers who ask her questions they would never dare ask their parents. "You're my friend," they say, "you'll understand."

They tell Judy about everything, from their innermost feelings to what happened in school. They also want to know about Judy. "Where do you get your ideas?" they ask. "Do you start with the characters, or the situation, or what? Did you always want to be a writer?"

She laughs at that question. Judy never dreamed of becoming a famous author. She never wrote down her thoughts on paper, but she did enjoy making up stories in her imagination. Now she can see that it was her love of storytelling that led to her profession as a writer. "Writing for me is just a continuation of a game of pretend. I was a very big pretender and still am, except now I act it out on paper."

Judy thinks a long time before she starts a new book. "Something will trigger an idea—maybe something I've read in the paper, maybe something I've heard, maybe a story I feel I want to tell. And then I walk around with it in my head for months, sometimes years."

She jots down ideas on whatever is handy—a Kleenex box next to her bed, scraps of paper in her purse. Then she sits down at the typewriter and begins to create the story. "I know something about my main character. I know where I am starting and where I am going. I usually don't know what's going to happen in between."

Her characters develop on paper as she works every day. By the time she finishes the first draft, they have become "real" people. "I tell a story by putting myself in the main character's shoes and ask how I would feel, what I would do, if this happened to me."

One of Judy's greatest strengths as a writer is her total recall. "I really do remember everything that's happened to me from the third grade on. I know just how I felt and exactly what I was thinking." She even remembers details—what dress she was wearing on a certain day, what the classroom smelled like. Such things help Judy relive a time in her childhood that she wants to tell a story about. Whatever it is happens to her all over again inside her head to give her stories the freshness of truth.

Judy is amazed that her career has turned out to be so successful. She didn't set out to become a best-selling author or break any barriers in children's literature. She simply wanted to write the kind of books that she would have enjoyed reading when she was young—books about kids as real people. "Kids have a right to read about themselves" says Judy. "They've been denied that right for a long time."

Judy Blume has become the champion of kids' rights, a hero to young readers everywhere. Books by Judy Blume have been translated into Dutch, Danish, and even Japanese. Her fourteen children's books have sold more than seven million copies, making her the most popular writer of juvenile fiction today. "I owe my career to my readers," says Judy.

Judy Blume has also received awards and honors from the publishing world. In 1978, when she addressed the American Booksellers Association Convention, she shared the platform with Dr. Seuss and Maurice Sendak, both of whom she had idolized when she was a beginning writer.

More important than anything else, her writing has brought her the freedom to be herself. Judy admits that for many years she lived a double life. First she was an anxious little girl trying to please her parents and later, a young woman trying to live up to her husband's expectations. Secretly, she was somebody else. Her deepest needs and feelings were locked inside of her.

Writing gave her a way to unlock the door of her secret dream life. As Judy shared that life with her readers, she came to know who she really was. And because she is honest enough to share her deepest feelings with kids, they open their hearts to her. "It's a rare, lovely relationship," she says. "They feel that they know me and I know them."

When Judy was growing up, she thought that she was the only one who felt alone and misunderstood. Now she knows that everyone feels alone sometimes—even adults. She wants kids to know that it's okay to feel that way, and that other people feel that way, too. Whatever the critics say, she feels that her main responsibility is to be true to herself and truthful to kids. As long as she does that, her books will be honest and daring and touch people's lives in a new way.